CHILDREN TIME.
POETRY TIME.

By: Shinary Nembhard

AuthorHouse™
1663 Liberty Drive
Bloomington, IN 47403
www.authorhouse.com
Phone: 833-262-8899

This book is printed on acid-free paper.

ISBN: 978-1-6655-3573-1 (sc)
ISBN: 978-1-6655-3572-4 (e)

Library of Congress Control Number: 2021917167

Print information available on the last page.

Published by AuthorHouse 08/23/2021

authorHOUSE®

Dedicated to my wonderful sister Britonya and my amazing little cousins Lavanne, Savanna, and Olianna. I love you all so much!

Table of Contents

SWEET BUTTERFLY.

Sweet butterfly flies in the sky but not too high and not too low.
Sweet butterfly kisses my face and shakes my hand.
Sweet butterfly lands on a flower, drinking its nectar.
Sweet butterfly plays with its friends flying in a circle.

OH, LITTLE RABBIT.

Oh, little rabbit sitting on the grass, staring at the trees.

Oh, little rabbit eating a carrot and leaving none for me.

Oh, little rabbit hop hop hop.

Oh, little rabbit if only you will stop.

THE TREE.

The tree dancing in the wind and smiling at the sun.

Branches stretch out like arms swaying side by side.

The leaves laugh and play as the rain tickles them.

DOWN BY THE RIVER.

Down by the river here we go.

Down by the river we soak our toes.

Down by the river we greet one another.

Down by the river we will always be together.

WHEN I AM MAD.

When I am mad, I stomp my feet.
When I am mad, I also feel sad.
When I am mad, I will cry.
When I am mad, my mom and my dad hug and kiss me,
To let me know that it is alright to feel mad.

LITTLE SISTERS.

Little sisters can be sweet

Little sisters can be rude

Little sisters can be amazing.

I have a little sister, but she never listens to me

I love my little sister and she loves me.

BIG BROTHERS.

I have a big brother who is big and strong,

my big brother loves to jump and run.

Plays with cards and plays with his cars.

My big brother loves to swim,

he loves the water so much maybe he is a fish.

I have a big brother who reads and writes,

Sometimes he teaches me how to spell.

I have a big brother who loves me very much and I love him.

SLEEPY SUN.

The sun bids the moon a good night as it settles in for rest.

The night has taken over as the day goes to sleep.

A new day starts when the sun rises again.

PUDDLES.

I love splashing in puddles

It's my favorite thing to do.

I even made up a song as I splash and splash.

"puddles, puddles, puddles, I love splashing you.

Puddles, puddles, puddles, you're my favorite thing to do."

HANDS AND FEET.

I've got ten fingers and ten toes
I can even touch my nose
I've got two eyes to see
And two ears to hear
One mouth to speak
And a head full of hair.

HAROLD SAILING THE SEAS.

Harold oh Harold sailing the seas
He discovers gum and he discovers cheese
Sailing in a boat from land to land
And country to country
Finally, he reaches me

DADDY AND I.

Daddy and I sipping a cup of tea
While sitting under our favorite tree
The stars are out and shining bright
And the moon is nowhere in sight
Dogs jump and play with fireflies
We gaze at the beauty of the skies
We take in all the wonders that are in our sight
Knowing that this night is going to be our night

SHAY WONDERS.

"Why do birds fly, and people walk?" Shay wonders, and "Why do fishes swim and worm slithers?"

"Why does the bee buzz and take the nectar of the flowers?" she ponders.

"Why are the grass green and the skies blue?"

"And why do I have five fingers on each hand, and five toes on each foot?"

Shay lies on a blanket in a field of grass, watching as the wind blows the leaves off the trees.

"Why do these things happen, and who is causing them to?"

"God made all things, great and small" her mother had once said. "He made the trees grow taller, and the grass greener, and the flowers have nectar for the buzzing bee. He made the fishes in the seas, and the worms in the earth. God made the skies blue; I don't know why." says her mother, "but he did. And do you know what else that God made, that is so special and dear to me?"

"No" shay shakes her head.

Her mother pulls her closer and kisses her forehead.

"You, my dear, he made you."

SAVVY AND LAVVY.

Savvy and Lavvy, playing hide and seek.
Savvy hid under the table in the living room,
While lavvy counted to ten.
"Ready are not, here I come," shouts Lavvy.
First, he looked under the bed, in the closet, behind the couch,
Then inside the pantry.
"Where is she?" Lavvy says.
Lavvy was about to give up when he heard Savvy's giggles coming
from the living room. Lavvy runs in there, scratching his head.
"But I searched in here," he says.
Yes, he did, but Lavvy did not look under the table.
He hears the giggles again, and follows the sound,
Where he sees Savvy's hands, covering her mouth trying to keep
Her giggles in.
"I found you," says lavvy
"Oh, how did you know where I was?"
"I just did. Now it's my turn to hide and your turn to count."
And the fun went on like that for the rest of the day.

BRITONYA AND HER BASKETBALL.

Britonya loves to play basketball.
It is one of her favorite sports.
She plays it in the morning before school,
She plays in the evening after school,
Britonya loves basketball so much,
It is one of her favorite things to do.

KITTY CAT!

Hello kitty cat!

     You with your brown and black spots,

With your curious bright brown eyes

     And your soft fur, that I cannot stop touching,

Watching my every move.

You stretch out on the sofa, licking your mouth

     Getting ready for your nap.

My wonderful kitty cat,

     I love you so much!

LIGHT.

Starlight

    Moonlight

        Shine upon us so bright

            Guiding us through the night

            To take away our fright

Now we know we'll be alright

OLIANNA.

Tip, tip, tip

Olianna tips down the hall

Trying to be quiet

And not to trip and fall

Balancing on her toes

Olianna sneaks up on her big sister and big brother

To scare them both.

"Gotcha" she says

And they jump laughing then fall.

AMAZED BY ALL THE THINGS THAT I CAN DO!

It is amazing that I can stand one foot

And write my name in different languages

And just amazing that I can help cook

My favorite food

And it is also amazing that I can sing

To my heart's content

It amazes me of all the things I can do

And so many more that I can try

And you what amazes me the most

Is this whole big world!

I am going to explore

Printed in the United States
by Baker & Taylor Publisher Services